RYA

GO WINDSURFING!

A practical handbook
for young people

RYA Go Windsurfing!

Words and Illustrations by: Claudia Myatt
Technical Editor: Amanda Van Santen

© Claudia Myatt 2013
First Published 2013

The Royal Yachting Association
RYA House
Ensign Way
Hamble
Southampton
SO31 4YA

Tel: 0844 556 9555
Fax: 0844 556 9516
E-mail: publications@rya.org.uk
Web: www.rya.org.uk
Follow us on Twitter @RYAPublications

ISBN: 978-1-906435042
RYA Order Code: G76

A CIP record of this book is available from the British Library.

Note: While all reasonable care has been taken in the preparation of this book, the publisher takes no responsibility for the use of the methods or products or contracts described in the book.

Totally Chlorine Free   Sustainable Forests

Cover Design: Claudia Myatt
Typeset: Creativebyte
Proofreading and indexing: Alan Thatcher
Printed through: World Print

FOREWORD

I started windsurfing when I was nine and I have always loved it. Whether it was blasting round a reservoir in Oxford or taking to the water in Beijing and Weymouth to compete in the Olympic Games, I've had a great time. I hope that this brilliant book will help you to learn about windsurfing so that you can have even more fun! Whether you want to race, do freestyle tricks or just enjoy yourself and make friends, windsurfing offers the chance to do all of these things. See you on the water!

Bryony Shaw
British Windsurfer and Olympic Bronze Medallist

CONTENTS

INTRODUCTION

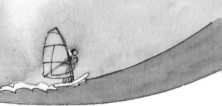

Like any sport, windsurfing is about practice, practice and more practice. It can seem difficult at first, but stick with it—soon you'll be flying across the water and you'll be hooked.

You can take it as far as you want to go; windsurf fast and win races, windsurf clever and learn amazing tricks, or just enjoy the magic of being out on the water and working in harmony with wind, sail and board.

So why do you need a book about it?

Reading this book before you start and while you're learning will save you time and frustration. Windsurfing involves your brain as well as your body. The more you understand about how the wind works, the more chance you have of staying safe, learning fast and getting the most from your time on the water.

Enjoy!

WHERE DO I START?

- Where can I learn?

- Boards and rigs

- Putting it all together

- Do I need a wetsuit?

- What else do I need?

When you stand on the shore watching experienced windsurfers flying over the waves, you think ,'I'd like to do that too!' But how? Where do you start?

Windsurfing is fast and fun—but you need the right kit, the right place and the right conditions to learn. Let's go!

The first step is to find a club or windsurfing centre that can teach beginners. Windsurfing is not a sport you can learn by yourself. You need to learn how the rig works, how to use wind and water and how to stay safe—and have plenty of fun along the way. It's also good to find friends to windsurf with and learn from.

RYA COURSES

Buying this book is a good start—and it's a good idea to get the RYA Youth Windsurfing Scheme logbook too.

Reading up about the basics first will help you understand what's happening when you get out on the water for real.

HOLIDAYS AND BEACH CLUBS

If you're lucky enough to have holidays somewhere sunny, persuade your family to go to a watersports or beach club resort which offers RYA windsurfing courses. The chances are there will be plenty of activities to keep the rest of the family busy so they don't have to sit and watch you!

SAILING CLUBS AND WINDSURFING CENTRES

You don't have to live near the sea to windsurf. There are many sailing and windsurfing centres on lakes as well as the coast—see if you can find one close by.

TEAM 15

If you can find a Team 15 club, then you're well on the way. Team 15 is a windsurfing club especially for under 15s, where you can learn in safety, have fun and learn to race against other T15 clubs if you want to.

www.team15.org.uk

Learning to windsurf doesn't cost a fortune. You don't need to buy a board and rig straight away—in fact it's best if you don't. When you take lessons at a windsurfing club or school you'll be able to learn about and try different types. Don't buy your own until you've got some experience and know what you need.

THE BOARD

Boards come in different shapes and sizes, but when you're starting out you need a wide, stable board with plenty of buoyancy.

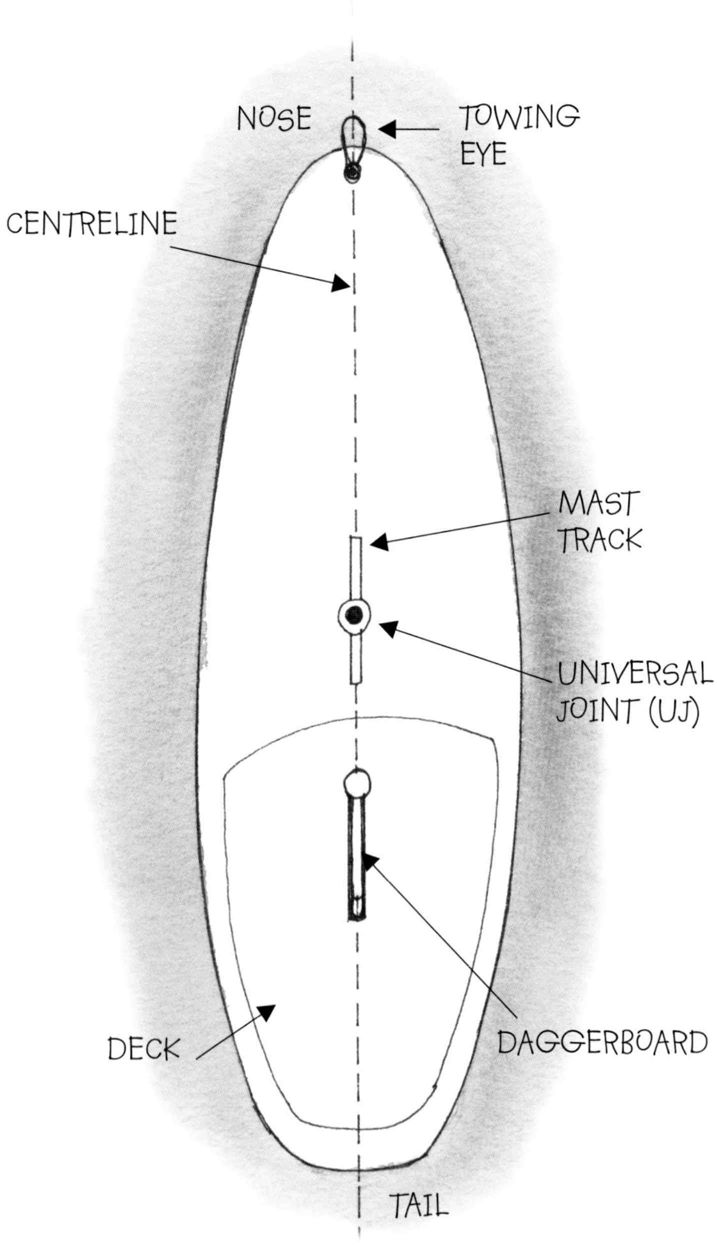

Top Tip

For your first lessons, the board and rig may be already assembled for you to use. Get someone to show you how to put it all together as soon as you get a chance, so that you can understand how it all works.

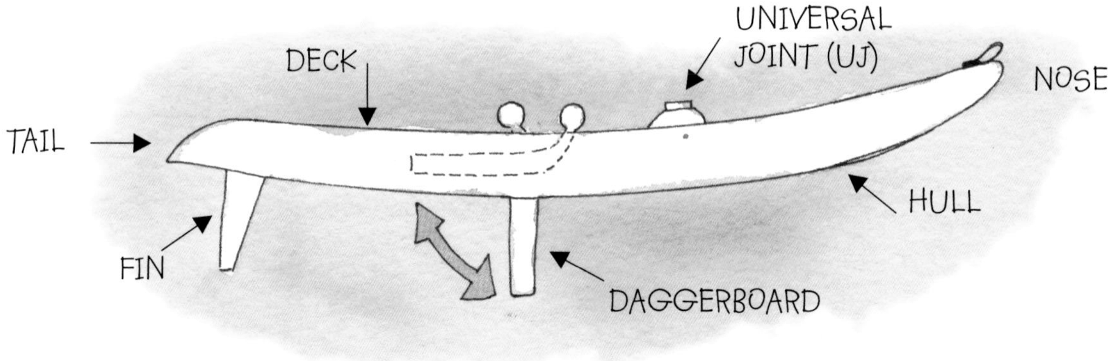

NOSE

TOWING EYE

CENTRELINE

MAST TRACK

UNIVERSAL JOINT (UJ)

DECK

DAGGERBOARD

TAIL

UNIVERSAL JOINT (UJ)

DECK

NOSE

TAIL

HULL

FIN

DAGGERBOARD

THE RIG

The windsurfer mast and sail is called the rig and, like the boards, the rig comes in all shapes and sizes. Small sails are for beginners and strong winds; big sails are for whizzy sailors or light winds.

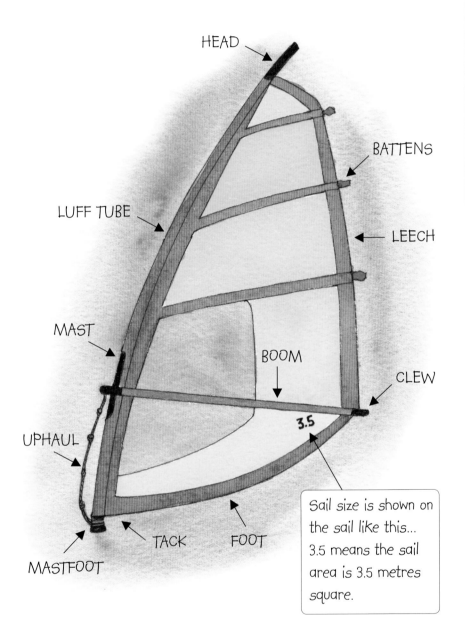

HEAD

BATTENS

LUFF TUBE

LEECH

MAST

BOOM

CLEW

3.5

UPHAUL

Sail size is shown on the sail like this... 3.5 means the sail area is 3.5 metres square.

TACK   FOOT

MASTFOOT

ADJUSTING THE BOOM

To make sure the boom is the right height, stand the rig upright. If the boom is not between your chest and shoulder, it will need adjusting—ask your instructor to show you how.

HOW BIG A SAIL?

It's important to use the right sail for your size and experience. Too big and the wind will pull it out of your hands; too small and you won't be able to feel the wind working. Your instructor will advise what's right for you.

When you first start to windsurf, the uphaul is the part of the rig that you'll be most familiar with, as it enables you to pull the sail up out of the water. For the first few lessons it might seem that's all you're doing, but stick with it.

When you start windsurfing lessons, the board and rig may be all ready to go. If it is, it's a good idea to learn how to rig your equipment as soon as you can. Soon you'll want to buy your own board so you need to be familiar with all the parts and how they fit together.

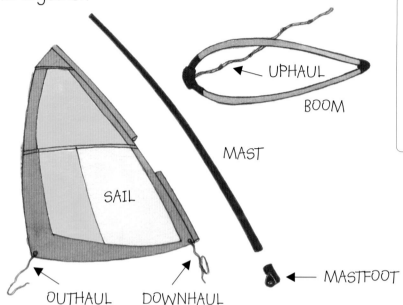

UPHAUL

BOOM

MAST

SAIL

OUTHAUL   DOWNHAUL

MASTFOOT

Lay everything out on the ground to make sure it's all there. Not all rigs are the same, so have a look at as many different types as you can to see how they're put together.

1. Slide the mast up the luff tube of the sail (thin end first).

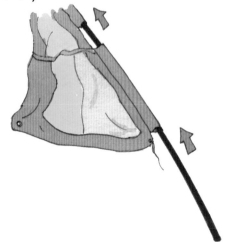

2. Put the mastfoot into the base of the mast, then attach the downhaul to the bottom of the sail. There will be a pulley system in the mastfoot to thread the downhaul through, but don't put too much tension on this for now.

3. Slide the boom onto the mast and clamp it tight. Don't worry about the boom height at this stage.

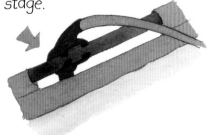

4. Thread the outhaul through the cleats at the outward end of the boom and through the eyelet on the sail. Don't put too much tension on it yet.

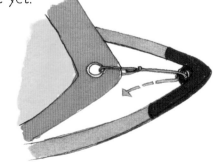

5. Now *back* to the downhaul, at the bottom of the sail. Give this a good pull until the tack of the sail is as close to the mastfoot as you can get it. This will take a bit of effort!

6. Now it's time to tighten the outhaul. Give this a good pull until the clew is next to the end of the boom.

7. Finally, stand the rig upright and *see* if it looks right. Make sure any loose ends of rope are tied off neatly.

If there are battens in the sail, tension them until any wrinkles disappear.

The clew of the sail should be as tight as possible against the end of the boom.

Check that the uphaul is attached to the mastfoot as well as to the front of the boom.

The tack of the sail should be as close as possible to the mastfoot.

The final stage—attaching the rig to the board—is best done close to the water. Find out how to do this in Chapter Three.

When you go for a swim, you stay in the water for a while and then come out and get dry, but when you windsurf you're in and out of the water all the time, especially as a beginner.

In a hot country this isn't a problem, but in cooler water you need the right gear to keep you warm.

HOW DO WETSUITS KEEP ME WARM?
Wetsuits work by keeping you wet! A well-fitting wetsuit traps a thin layer of water inside which is kept warm by your body heat. If the wetsuit is too big, cold water will come sloshing in through the gaps around your neck, wrist and ankles—yeuk! But if it's too tight, your movements will be restricted.

It can be a problem when you're growing fast and have to keep buying the next size up, but if you join a club with other youngsters it should be possible to trade with each other and develop a second-hand wetsuit market. You can borrow a wetsuit from the centres and clubs you learn at.

BAD IDEA

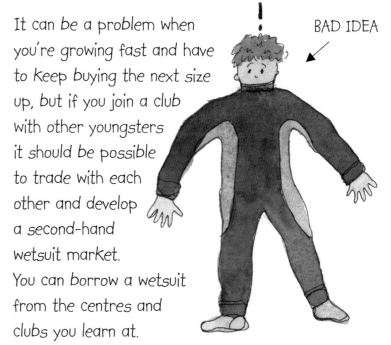

WHAT SORT DO I NEED?
Which sort you buy depends on what kind of weather and water conditions you'll be sailing in.

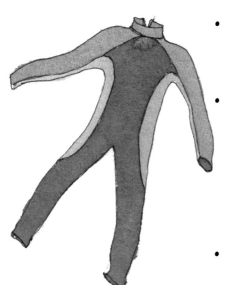

- A winter wetsuit is called a steamer —it has long legs and arms and is made of 5mm-thick neoprene.
- A summer suit (or shortie) has short sleeves and legs and is lightweight (2mm thick) for warmer weather. You may already have one of these for messing around on the beach.
- Between these two types you can also get a convertible suit—about 3mm thick and sometimes with detachable arm pieces.

What else do you need besides a wetsuit? Here are a few extras that will help you stay out on the water longer and windsurf in cooler weather...

RASH VESTS

A thin top worn under a wetsuit for extra comfort—can also be worn on its own on days when you don't need a wetsuit, for extra protection. You can also buy UV protection rash vests for hot days.

HAT

For really cold winter days you can wear a neoprene hat or helmet, especially designed for windsurfing. Make sure any headgear fits well and doesn't restrict your movements.

WETSUIT BOOTS

You can windsurf in bare feet, but in cold water wetsuit boots are a good idea. They'll keep your feet warm, give you a good grip on the board and are especially good if you sail from a stony beach!

GLOVES

Windsurfing gloves give you extra warmth and grip in cold weather.

Top Tip

Look after your wetsuit! Rinse it in fresh water after you've used it, then hang it up—don't keep it crunched up in your sailing bag. Keep the zip in good shape by occasionally rubbing zip lubricant on it.

STAY WARM

It's always colder on the water than on shore—make sure you're properly kitted out for the kind of weather you're out in.

What else do you need? And what about hot weather windsurfing? It's great to be able to jump onto a board in your swimming gear and enjoy falling in the water for a cool down, but there are still things you need to think about...

BUOYANCY AIDS

Wherever you windsurf, you'll need a buoyancy aid—even if you think you're a strong swimmer. A buoyancy aid is designed to help you stay afloat in the water. All centres will provide you with one.

Some buoyancy aids have a zip-up compartment at the front, which is useful—but only put stuff in there that you don't mind getting wet!

DINGHY BOOTS

Bare feet are fine for windsurfing in hot weather—but you might find lightweight boots give you a better grip (and protect your feet from hot sand or shingle!).

sizzle

sizzle

Don't get dehydrated! Keep a bottle of drink handy and remember to use it.

Sun cream will get washed off in the sea, so wear a tee-shirt as well to protect you from sunburn.

SUN SAFE

GET THE RIGHT FIT

A buoyancy aid is no good if it doesn't fit you properly. If it's too big, it will slip up over your head when you fall in the water.

Set up a swapshop at your windsurfing club to buy and sell wetsuits and buoyancy aids as you grow out of them. If you do buy a second-hand buoyancy aid, make sure it's in good condition.

BAD IDEA

Rigged and ready to go? Windsurfing is about three things—wind, windsurfer and you. So before getting out on the wet stuff, let's take a closer look at the windy stuff...

WILD ABOUT WIND

- Which way is it blowing?

- How windy is it?

- Understanding the forecast

- Local effects

Wind is the invisible free fuel that makes a board fly, so it's not surprising that a windsurfer is obsessed by wind. You gaze out of the window and watch the leaves rustling on the trees. All the good weather forecast websites are on your 'favourites' list. You know the difference between offshore and onshore winds and how sea breezes work.

Wind awareness is something you can practise and learn about before you even get on the water—and if you do, what happens on the water starts to make sense a lot sooner...

For a windsurfer, the DIRECTION of the wind is vitally important. The first thing to do when you get down to the water's edge is turn your face to the wind. Where's it coming from? Is it ONSHORE, OFFSHORE, or somewhere in between?

ONSHORE WIND

This means the wind blows from sea to land. If you get into difficulties, the wind will always blow you back to the shore. The downside is that there may be waves breaking onto the beach, so when setting off you may need to paddle the board into calmer waters to stop the wind blowing you back onto the beach.

WIND

OFFSHORE WIND

This means the wind blows from land to sea. It's easy to get going, as the beach will be nice and calm and the wind will blow you quickly away from the shore. But beware—until you're able to steer the board into the wind, you'll find it very hard to get back. Even experienced windsurfers avoid an offshore wind.

WIND

WATCH OUT !

CROSS-SHORE WIND

If the wind is blowing across the beach, life is much easier. You can sail to and fro across the bay on the easiest point of sail—across the wind. But be aware that the wind will gradually blow you down the beach—so watch out if there are rocks or other hazards downwind.

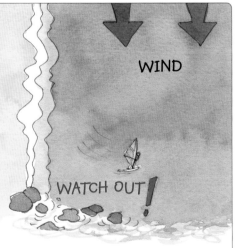

WIND

WATCH OUT !

Top Tip

Not sure which way the wind is blowing? A training centre will usually have a flag flying on the beach—a quick look at this will tell you everything you need to know.

RYA

It's important to know the strength of the wind as well as the direction. Your level of experience will determine how much wind is too much—when starting out, you'll be sailing in gentle breezes and leaving the strong winds to the experts!

HOW DO WE MEASURE WIND STRENGTH?

Back in the 19th century a clever sailor called Admiral Beaufort made up the Beaufort Scale to help sailors work out wind strength by observing the state of the sea and waves. With a few changes, it's still used in shipping forecasts today. This is what it means for you...

Force 0—CALM No wind at all, sea flat like a mirror. Practise rigging your equipment, read this book, and watch out for ripples on the water that show wind is on its way.

Force I—LIGHT AIRS (1-3 knots of wind) Small ripples on the water. It's a good time to get on the water and start practising.

Force 2—LIGHT BREEZE (4-6 knots of wind) Small wavelets, no breaking crests. This is a good breeze to get the feel of the sail without the wind trying to pull it out of your hands.

Force 3—GENTLE BREEZE (7-10 knots of wind) Bigger wavelets, with a few white crests. Once you get a bit more confident, you'll find this a good fast breeze, but if it's too much to begin with, try a smaller sail.

Force 4—MODERATE BREEZE (11–16 knots of wind) Waves have more frequent white crests. Beginners head for shore and experienced sailors come out to play.

Force 6 and over (more than 22 knots) A full gale begins at 35 knots of wind and goes right up to Hurricane at Force 12!

Hmm... force 10 or 11?

Force 5—FRESH BREEZE (17–21 knots) Waves are bigger, with white crests and a chance of spray. Don't even think about tackling a wind like this just yet.

If it's too windy to sail, you can learn from watching experienced windsurfers. One day you'll be out there too!

KNOT

NOT A KNOT

WHEN IS A KNOT NOT A KNOT?
Maritime weather forecasts use knots as a measure of wind speed. A knot is a nautical mile per hour, and a nautical mile is a bit longer than a land mile. But many forecasts use kilometres per hour or miles per hour instead of knots, which can get confusing. At the back of this book there's a chart that converts all these different measurements into the Beaufort Scale.

Top Tip
Practise trying to work out the strength of the wind by observation—then check online to see how close you were!

A basic idea of how weather patterns work will help you get the most out of a forecast and give you some idea of what to expect on the water. The more you understand weather, the easier it will be to work out when the conditions are right for windsurfing.

HIGH OR LOW?
Two types of weather patterns determine whether or not we're able to sail...

RAINY BITS

In the northern hemisphere, wind blows CLOCKWISE around a high-pressure system and ANTI-CLOCKWISE around a low-pressure system (opposite in the southern hemisphere).

HIGH PRESSURE
High pressure (anticyclone) brings settled, dry weather.

This often means light winds, unless the high-pressure system is squeezed between areas of low to produce strong, steady breezes. But if not, don't despair—high pressure in summer can lead to afternoon sea breezes.

LOW PRESSURE
Low pressure (depression) brings unsettled weather, often with bands of rain and wind called weather fronts. The wind direction will change in both strength and direction as the weather fronts (rainy bits) pass through.

HOW DO WEATHER CHARTS SHOW WIND?
Weather maps are called synoptic charts. Lines called isobars join up areas of equal air pressure, like the contour lines on a map. The closer the lines on a map, the steeper the hill; the closer the isobars, the stronger the wind.

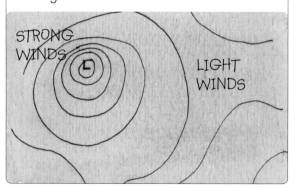

STRONG WINDS

LIGHT WINDS

WHAT DO THE WORDS IN THE FORECAST MEAN?
The words in the shipping forecast have very exact meanings. If a gale is described as 'imminent', how long before it arrives? If the wind is easing to a force 3 'soon', does that mean you can rush down to the beach?

IMMINENT—means within six hours.
SOON—means between six to twelve hours' time.
LATER—means after twelve hours.

Is supper 'imminent'?

It's never been easier to find out what the wind and weather is doing, or going to do. TV, radio or internet will all provide forecasts, as well as the notice board of your windsurf shop or training centre.

Amongst all this information, how do you find out what you need to know?

THE MET OFFICE

The study of weather is called METEOROLOGY, and the Meteorological Office is the source for most other sites' forecasts.

If you're windsurfing on the coast, go to www.metoffice.gov.uk and look for the marine forecast. The INSHORE WATERS forecast is the most useful to find out what the wind is doing around your patch of coast.

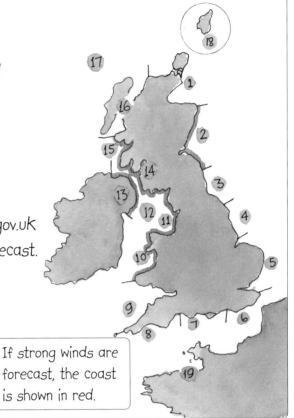

If strong winds are forecast, the coast is shown in red.

WIND DIRECTION

The forecast tells you wind direction as well as strength. For example, 'Southwesterly force 4' means that the wind will be coming FROM the south-west at between 11 and 15 knots (Force 4).

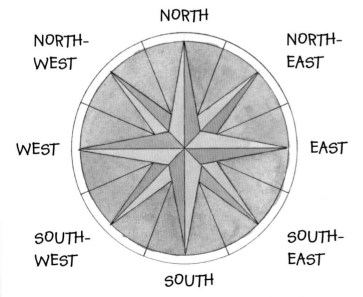

Find out which way your windsurfing beach faces. Then you'll know whether a 'Southwesterly force 4' means that you have an offshore or onshore wind.

SMARTY PANTS TIP
Want to impress your friends with your weather knowledge? Stand with your back to the wind, and if you're in the northern hemisphere you can tell them that the centre of low pressure is over to the left. In the southern hemisphere, low pressure is to your right.

The weather forecast will give you a general idea of what the wind is likely to do, but it rarely blows steadily from one direction, even out at sea. The land around you bends and shapes the wind, so learn to watch out for the signs...

LOCAL WINDS

Get to know your sailing area. On a lake, hills and woodland can interrupt the flow of wind so that you get calm bits and gusts.

Stronger winds here...

Wobbly winds here...

TRICKY BITS

At sea, it can often *be* sheltered in a bay and much windier off headlands.

Winds can *be* particularly turbulent around high cliffs, so don't get too close.

eek!

SEA BREEZES

In hot weather, you often get calm conditions in the morning and a stronger wind in the afternoon. This is called a *sea breeze* and this is why it happens....

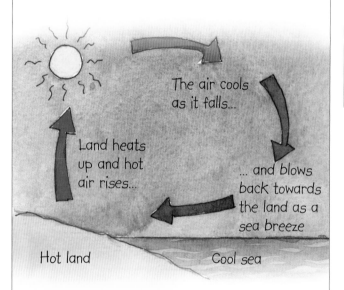

The air cools as it falls...

Land heats up and hot air rises...

... and blows back towards the land as a sea breeze

Hot land

Cool sea

If you are taking windsurfing lessons on holiday in a hot country, you'll find the beginner courses are likely to be in the morning to give you the gentlest winds.

WATCH THE WATER

An experienced windsurfer can spot a dark patch of rippled water that shows a gust of wind is on its way. Learn to recognise the signals and you won't get caught out!

tee hee

Top Tip

When looking up the weather forecast, try and get information that's as local as possible. Some coastal areas have their own weather stations, which means you can look online and get an accurate wind reading as it happens.

WILD ABOUT WATER

- Carrying the rig and board

- Secure position

- Static turn

- Sailing!

- All about stance

- Stopping and getting help

When you first get on a windsurfer, everything wobbles—the board, the water and you! For the first few tries it might feel that you're in the water more than you're on the board, but stick with it; all that falling in is part of the fun and you'll soon get better!

Rigged up and ready to go? Is your sail the right size and the boom adjusted for your height? First you need to get your board and rig to the water...

CARRYING THE RIG

The rig is light but can be awkward to carry if you don't take the wind direction into account. Stand with your back to the wind and pick up the rig using boom and mast...

Then walk to the water, keeping your back to the wind. But if you put the rig down on the beach it might blow away, so the safest way is to put it in the water briefly while you go back for the board.

CARRYING THE BOARD

Boards are heavy, so team up and carry an end each.

An adult can carry a board on their own by rolling it onto its side then lifting it with one hand on the daggerboard and one on the daggerboard handle.

If you need to leave the attached rig and board on the beach, leave the board upside down on the rig like this...

NOW PUT THEM TOGETHER

With board and rig in the water, push the mastfoot into the universal joint (UJ) until you hear it connect.

click!

Now you're ready to go!

Top Tip
It's not a good idea to drag the board down to the water, especially if it's a stony beach. But if you do need to drag it a short distance, pick it up at the tail so you don't damage the fin.

Now for the fun bit—getting wet! The first stage is to get onto the board, find your balance and get the sail out of the water ready to go. This is called the SECURE POSITION...

1. Stand in thigh-deep water and put the daggerboard down. Line the board up across the wind so that your back is to the wind and the rig is lying on the downwind side.

2. Put your hands over the centreline and pull yourself up until you are kneeling on the board.

3. Grab hold of the uphaul to help you hold on.

4. Making sure the wind is still behind you, stand up with a straight back and your feet either side of the mastfoot. Bend your knees, lean back against the uphaul and pull the rig partly out of the water. Straighten up as you do this so that your legs, not your back, do the pulling.

5. Move your hands one at a time up the uphaul so that the rig gently rises out of the water. Hold it there for a moment.

Then move one hand at a time onto the mast, just below the boom.

Keep your arms extended and your head up, so there's a V-shape between you and the rig.

Keep your knees slightly bent to help balance you.

Top Tip

Remember to check that the daggerboard is down before you get going. How do you tell? The handle will be at the back of the slot when the board is down.

BACK   FRONT

6. Still standing? Hooray, you are now in the **SECURE POSITION!**

7. Oops. Well, you were in the secure position! Now have another go.

tee hee!

If you end up in the water with your rig facing upwind, don't worry. Climb onto the board and start to lift the rig out of the water. Then wait until the wind catches under the sail and gently swings the board around. Once you have your back to the wind again, carry on pulling the sail up as before.

WIND

I'm getting the hang of the insecure position...

Remember to use the skills you learnt earlier when *balancing on the board* to help you in the secure position.

wibble wobble

wibble wobble

The next step is called a **STATIC TURN**. Turning the board through 180 degrees is the beginning of learning to steer the board and take control. Here's how...

1. Start by getting into the secure position, with your *back* to the wind.

2. Gently tilt the rig to the BACK of the board. The front of the board will start to turn into the wind.

3. This is the clever bit—the board will move, but you need to stay in the same place!

Take little steps around the mastfoot to keep your back to the wind as the board moves round under you.

4. Keep the rig tilted back and moving across the board—keep your arms extended—until the board has turned completely round 180° and is facing the opposite way.

5. Now you're back in the secure position—well done!
If you managed that without falling in, *see* if you can complete the turn and end up where you started. Lean the rig to the back of the board and shuffle round again as the board turns.

Top Tip
If you get in a muddle, go back to the secure position, make sure the wind is blowing onto your back, then try again.

Now *see* if you can turn the board in the opposite direction...

1. Starting from the secure position, tilt the rig towards the FRONT of the board. This time the front of the board will turn downwind.

2. Move around the mast with tiny steps as the board turns. Keep the rig tilted until the board has turned 180 degrees.

3. Now get back to the secure position.
Well done, you've turned the board completely round in both directions!
Carry on round until you are back where you started.

The further you tilt the rig, the faster the board will turn. See how fast you can do the static turn without falling in!

WHICH WAY DO I TURN?

How do you work out which way to tilt the rig to make the board turn? You'll soon get used to it, but try and remember that the part of the board you lean the rig over is the part that the wind will turn downwind.

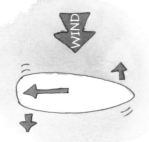

Remember that tipping the rig back steers you TOWARDS the direction the wind is blowing.

Tipping the rig forward steers you DOWNWIND.

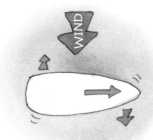

Ready to start **SAILING**? Let's take the next step—from the secure position to sailing across the wind.

1. Start in the secure position. Think about where the wind is coming from. Aim your eyes at a goal to sail for **across** the wind.

2. Take your front hand off the mast and onto the boom.

4. Shuffle your back foot until it's behind the daggerboard handle, across the centreline.

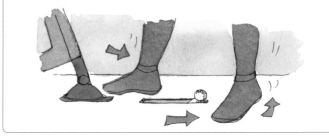

3. When you're ready, move the other hand off the mast. Now you're holding onto the rig with one hand at the mast end of the boom.

Top Tip
Don't look down at your feet! Keep your head up and your eyes on your goal.

5. Now turn your shoulders to face the front of the board and your goal. At the same time, pull the rig across the board to the point where it feels light and easy to hold—this is the **BALANCE POINT**. At the same time, bend your back leg and drop your body back and down until you feel balanced.

6. Now place your back hand on the boom and slowly pull the sail in. You'll feel the pressure of the wind come onto the sail.

Splosh!
Oops... well, you were sailing. Get back on and have another go!

DON'T FORGET!
Stay aware of WIND DIRECTION.
During this lesson, you're trying to keep the wind coming over the side of the board.

7. Using your body to balance the weight of wind in the sail, keep your head up and eyes on your goal.

If you don't feel comfortable, move your hands and feet until you are.
Hooray, you're sailing!

Top Tip
If the wind is offshore, keep an eye on how far you are from the beach. When you're concentrating hard, it's easy to lose track of how far you've been blown downwind.

As soon as the wind fills the sail and you use your body to balance it, you become part of the machine. Whether you move smoothly across the water in the direction you want to go or fall in with a big splash depends on one important thing—**STANCE**.

WHAT IS STANCE? Stance is all about you—the way you stand on the board and hold the rig. A good sailing stance should look something like this...

ARMS—extended so the rig feels comfortable. Hands shoulder width apart—you should feel equal pressure in both arms.

GOOD STANCE

HEAD—facing the direction you're going. Look ahead—not just at the point you're sailing towards but at anything you might be about to crash into!

BODY—relaxed and comfortable, continuously moving to balance board and rig.

MOVEMENT—smooth and flowing.

LEGS—fairly straight but don't ever lock your knees. Front foot facing forward, back foot across the board. Drop down on the back knee if you're having trouble balancing the rig in stronger winds.

V is for 'Very Good!'
When your stance is right, there will be a V shape between your body and the rig, like this...

Top Tip
In stronger winds, drop your body lower by bending the back knee to help balance the pressure in the sail.

There's a lot to remember when you're starting out, and you can't *see* what you look like when your stance is wrong, can you? Here's a picture that might help. If you're falling off more than moving forward, this could be you...

ARMS—bent close to the boom, or stretching out too far. Hands gripping too tightly, or too close together, or too far apart. Arms could be the right width apart, but too far forward or too far back.

HEAD—looking at your feet, at the rig... anywhere but at your goal.

BAD STANCE

BODY—bottom sticking out as you try to pull against the weight of wind in the rig. Bending at the waist is a really bad idea.

LEGS—tense with the effort of not falling in. Knees are locked and have forgotten how to flex.

Feet might not be on the centreline.

MOVEMENT— jerky and wobbly!

O is for 'Oh dear!'
When your stance is wrong, there might be an O shape between your body and the rig, like this...

Top Tip
Be aware of how much wind there is as well as its direction. If the wind keeps snatching the sail out of your hands and you have trouble balancing the rig, try a smaller sail.

Now you've started sailing, how do you stop safely? You'll be pleased to know there are other ways to stop besides falling off!

STOP SLOWLY

To slow down and stop gently, just take your back hand off the boom and return to the secure position.

STOP QUICKLY...

If you need to put the brakes on quickly, release your back hand and lower the rig into the water. Crouch down onto the board as you do it and you'll come to a fast stop without falling in.

Top Tip
When stopping at the beach, try and remember to raise the daggerboard, using your foot on the daggerboard handle.

HELP!

What happens if you've been blown too far downwind and can't sail back? Try being a butterfly—lay the rig over the back of the board like this, lying face down with your feet resting on the sail. Now use your hands to paddle back to shore. Aim for the nearest land rather than trying to paddle back to the place you set off.

HELP!

If you're too tired or too far from shore to be able to rescue yourself, kneel on the board and slowly raise and lower your arms. This is a recognised distress signal to summon help.

Top Tip
Always, always stay with the board—it will keep you afloat until you're rescued or make it to shore.

Also, it's a lot easier for a rescuer to spot than a head in the water.

There's a lot more about safety in Chapter Five.

TAKING CONTROL

- Points of sail

- How to steer

- Steering downwind

- Tacking

- Sailing downwind

- Gybing

Now you're getting the hang of sailing, the next step is to take control of the board and rig, learn to steer and turn without stopping.

So far, you've been sailing to and fro across the wind. This is a good place to start, but now it's time to learn how to sail in other directions relative to the wind. Here's a seagull's eye view of all the 'points of sail'...

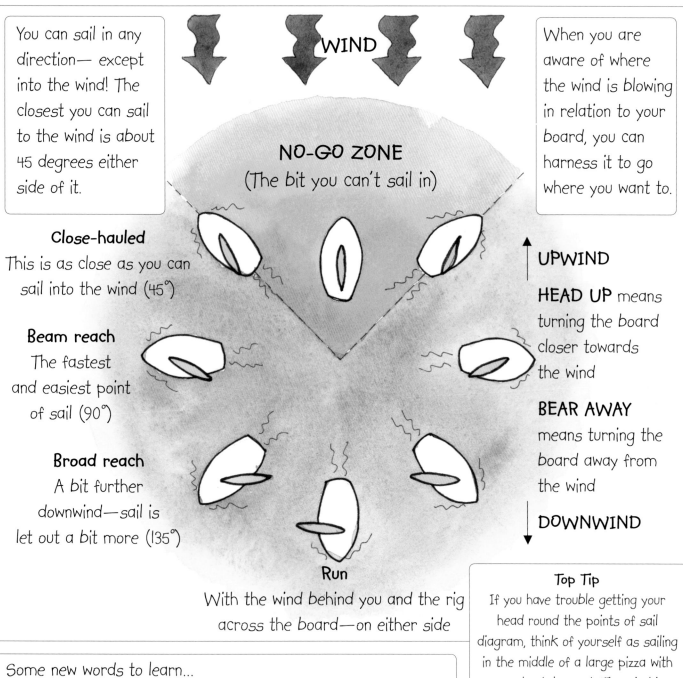

You can sail in any direction— except into the wind! The closest you can sail to the wind is about 45 degrees either side of it.

WIND

NO-GO ZONE
(The bit you can't sail in)

When you are aware of where the wind is blowing in relation to your board, you can harness it to go where you want to.

Close-hauled
This is as close as you can sail into the wind (45°)

Beam reach
The fastest and easiest point of sail (90°)

Broad reach
A bit further downwind—sail is let out a bit more (135°)

Run
With the wind behind you and the rig across the board—on either side

UPWIND

HEAD UP means turning the board closer towards the wind

BEAR AWAY means turning the board away from the wind

DOWNWIND

Some new words to learn...

STARBOARD TACK means the wind is coming over the right-hand side of the board (and your right hand is at the front of the boom).

PORT TACK means the wind is coming over the left-hand side of the board (your left hand is at the front of the boom).

Top Tip
If you have trouble getting your head round the points of sail diagram, think of yourself as sailing in the middle of a large pizza with a wedge taken out. The wind is blowing into the wedge, and that's the bit you can't sail in!

Windsurfing— yummy!

You steer a boat with a tiller or a wheel—but how do you steer a windsurfer? The secret is in the position of the rig. Remember tilting the rig towards the back of the board when doing the static turn? Now you'll learn how to do that on the move.

TURNING UPWIND

1. Get yourself sailing across the wind, then choose a new goal to aim for which is slightly closer to the wind...

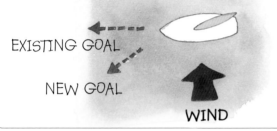

EXISTING GOAL

NEW GOAL

WIND

2. Keep your eyes on your new goal, and tilt the rig towards the back of the board. To do this your front arm will bend more and your back arm will straighten.

3. When the nose of your board is pointing in the new direction, bring the rig back to the sailing position.

4. Use your back hand to bring the sail slightly closer in to the board when sailing close to the wind.

HOW IT LOOKS

This is a seagull's eye view of your change of direction...

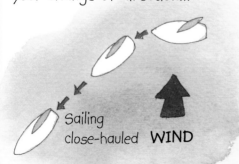

Sailing close-hauled WIND

WHAT WENT WRONG?

If you find it hard to get moving again after turning towards the wind, you may have turned too far and gone into the no-go zone. Remember you can only sail at about 45 degrees to the wind.

Just right

Oops, too far! You're in the no-go zone. WIND

TURNING DOWNWIND

1. Choose a new goal to aim for—ideally the one you were sailing towards before you turned upwind.

NEW GOAL

EXISTING GOAL

WIND

3. When the nose of the board is pointing across the wind again, bring the rig back to the sailing position.

How do you know how far to pull the sail in or out when you change direction?

The more you turn towards the wind, the closer you pull the rig to the board. When you turn downwind, you gradually let the rig out to catch more wind. Look at the diagram on page 39 which gives you an idea of where the rig should be for each point of sail.

BEAM REACH

CLOSE-HAULED

WIND

2. Keep your eyes on your new goal and move the rig across your body towards the front of the board. To do this, you'll be extending your front arm and bringing your back arm closer to your face.

4. With your back arm, let the sail out slightly, back to its original sailing position.

Once you've practised steering in one direction, turn round and have a go on the other tack!

Turning the board through the 'eye' of the wind is called **TACKING**. Both you and the rig have to swap sides, but don't worry, it's not as tricky as it sounds. It's a bit like the static turn, when you tilted the rig to the back of the board, but now you need to learn to do it smoothly and on the move!

1. From sailing a course across the wind, look directly into the wind—this is the way you're going to go. To do this, you need to steer and sail the board slightly closer to the wind—close-hauled.

2. From close-hauled, tilt the rig to the back of the board. As the board turns towards the wind, move your front hand off the boom and onto the mast just below the boom.

3. As soon as you enter the no-go zone, the board will slow down. Bring your back foot in front of the mast and your other hand off the boom onto the mast.

Top Tip
Keep the rig tilted back as the board moves—it can help to imagine you are trying to sweep a crab off the end of the board!

4. Take steps round the mastfoot to the other side of the board. The board will now be facing in the new direction and you will be back in the secure position.

5. Make sure your feet are in the right position for sailing, then move your hands back onto the boom.

6. Pull the sail in until you feel the pull of the wind, and off you go on the new tack! You should be sailing in the opposite direction to when you started.

Top Tip
If you get confused, stop and think about where the wind is coming from and where you are on the points of sail diagram.

NO-GO ZONE

SAILING TOWARDS THE WIND

Practise tacking until you can move smoothly from one side of the wind to the other without stopping.

Got it? Now try zig-zagging as close to the no-go zone as you can on each tack. This is the secret of being able to sail upwind!

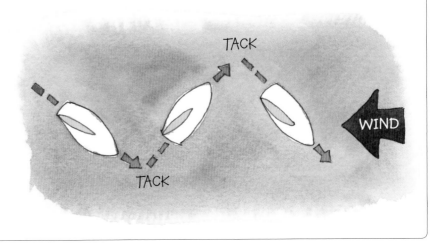

TACK

TACK

WIND

So far all your sailing has been done in the top half of the points of sail diagram—across the wind, upwind and tacking across the no-go zone. Now it's time to turn the board downwind...

SAILING DOWNWIND

You'd think sailing downwind would be easy, but in fact it can be tricky. There is more power in the sail when the wind is pushing you along, and it can feel much harder to control. The wobbliest point of sailing is directly downwind, so it is usually easier to go from broad reach to broad reach.

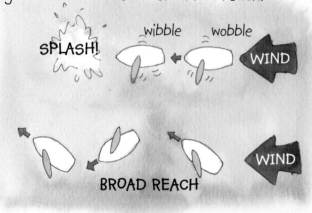

1. Start by sailing on a beam reach and look for a new goal point away from the wind.

2. Move your back hand further towards the end of the boom.

3. Then tilt the rig towards the front of the board, just like you did on page 31.

4. As the board turns, drop lower on your back knee to balance the rig. Once the board is aiming for your new goal point, bring the rig back to the sailing position, **but** ease out the sail with your back hand.

The next step is turning the board downwind so that the wind is coming from the other side of the sail—this is called **GYBING**.

HOW TO GYBE

When you TACK, you bring the nose of the board into the wind through the no-go zone. A **GYBE** is the opposite—a downwind turn, so there isn't a no-go zone. You don't have to change sides this time, just do a nifty bit of shuffling to swap your feet and hands. Here's how...

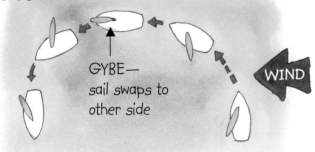

GYBE—
sail swaps to
other side

WIND

1. Sail a broad reach and tilt the rig forward until the nose of the board is pointing directly downwind and ease out with your back hand.

2. Move your front foot back to just behind the centreboard like this...

...then bring your back foot forward, into the new sailing position.

3. Slide your front hand up towards the mast and drop the back hand. At this point the rig will be swinging free over the front of the board with no weight of wind in it.

4. Reach across your body with your free hand and grab the boom on the other side...

Now your other hand can take up its new position halfway down the boom. Well done, you have brought the sail round to the other side!

5. Get into the sailing position and head for your new goal point. Well done, you've gybed successfully!

Now try and gybe back the other way...

If you have trouble balancing the weight of wind in the sail, keep your weight low by shuffling your back foot further to the back of the board and bending your knee.

Top Tip
Don't bend at the waist when you feel the extra pull on the sail downwind. Lower your weight by bending the back knee instead.

oops!

BAD IDEA

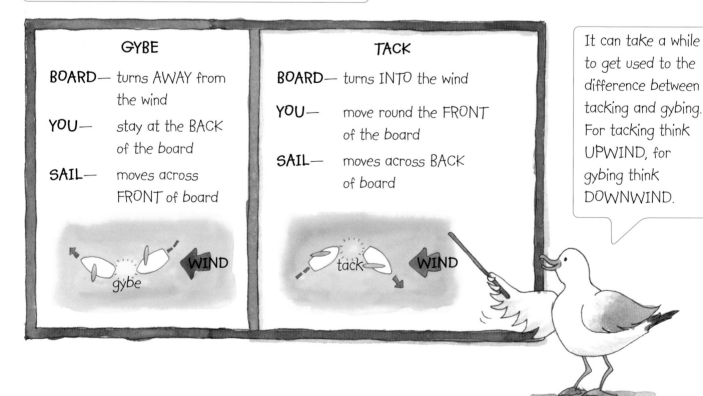

GYBE

BOARD— turns AWAY from the wind

YOU— stay at the BACK of the board

SAIL— moves across FRONT of board

gybe   WIND

TACK

BOARD— turns INTO the wind

YOU— move round the FRONT of the board

SAIL— moves across BACK of board

tack   WIND

It can take a while to get used to the difference between tacking and gybing. For tacking think UPWIND, for gybing think DOWNWIND.

SEA SENSE

- The seven common senses

- All about tides

- Avoiding collisions

- Help!

- Knotty knots

Wind awareness is just one of the *sea senses* a windsurfer needs. You may not *be* going far from the shore, but you *still* need to develop a sailor's instinct and respect for the water. A bit of careful preparation can leave you free to enjoy yourself without getting caught out, especially as you increase confidence and want to spread your wings.

What do you need to do to stay safe on the water? As a beginner you'll be learning in a safe place with help close by, but it's never too soon to start thinking like a pro...

THE SEVEN COMMON SENSES CHECKLIST

1. Is all your equipment seaworthy and suitable? Make sure you wear suitable clothing. At a minimum, wetsuit, boots and a buoyancy aid should be worn. Check the mastfoot for signs of wear. The rubber or hinged part of the mastfoot should have a built-in safety strap to keep the rig attached to the board in the event of it breaking. Check that all the ropes are secure and in good condition and that the sail is free from splits or tears. Masts and booms should be checked for signs of wear and replaced if necessary. Carry some spare line for your outhaul/downhaul and a means of attracting attention (a Dayglo flag and/or a whistle). **Remember, the most common need for rescue is equipment failure!**

2. Tell someone where you are going and when you will be back. It is recommended that you always windsurf at a location that has safety provision. Always ensure that a responsible person knows that you have gone out on the water, what time you expect to be back, and that you remember to tell them when you have returned.

3. Obtain a weather forecast for the local sailing area. This will prevent you getting caught in changing conditions. If you are sailing at a new location seek advice from experienced local windsurfers.

4. Are you capable of handling the prevailing conditions? Ensure that you can deal with the conditions that you are going out in. Developing your skills in more challenging conditions should take place at a safe location which ideally has safety provision. **If in doubt, don't go out!**

5. Windsurf with others. It is more fun to windsurf with other people. Not only will you learn from each other but also there will be somebody close should you need help.

6. Avoid strong tides, offshore winds and poor visibility. Offshore winds and tidal streams can sweep you away. It is essential that you understand the conditions you are windsurfing in and any dangers that may be present. Windsurfing in poor visibility should be avoided because you cannot see any dangers or landmarks and it prevents others from seeing you if you get into difficulty.

7. Consider other water-users. Many windsurfing locations are used by other water-users, so always respect each other by giving them space and take the necessary action to avoid a collision.

Top Tip
Make your own safety-check poster for your sailing-club wall.

If you learn on non-tidal water, it can be a shock to sail on the sea and find out just how much difference tides can make. Tides are stronger on some parts of the coast than others, but you need to understand how they work and how they can affect you.

WHAT CAUSES TIDES?

You already know that tides are caused by the pull of the sun and moon. But do you know the difference between spring and neap tides?

SPRING TIDES happen when the sun and moon are in line—full and new moon—so the pull is stronger. When sun and moon are pulling in different directions the pull is weaker, and these are **NEAP TIDES**. There are two spring tides and two neap tides every month, which is the time it takes the moon to go round the earth.

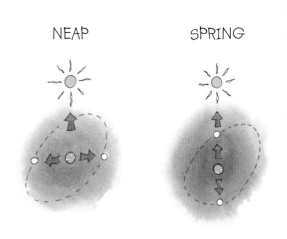

NEAP   SPRING

HOW OFTEN DOES THE TIDE GO IN AND OUT?

There are two high and two low tides every day, so it takes just over six hours for the tide to flow between high and low. If you buy a tide table for your local area, you can work out what the tide is doing at any time.

A tide table can look confusing, but this is what all the numbers mean...

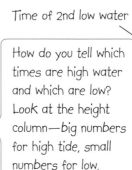

How do you tell which times are high water and which are low? Look at the height column—big numbers for high tide, small numbers for low.

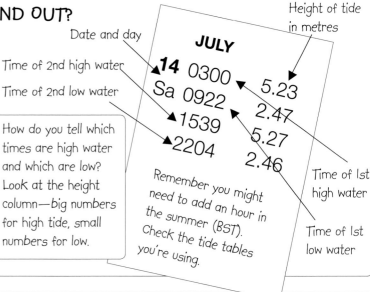

Date and day

Time of 2nd high water

Time of 2nd low water

Height of tide in metres

JULY

14 0300 → 5.23

Sa 0922 → 2.47

1539 → 5.27

2204 → 2.46

Time of 1st high water

Time of 1st low water

Remember you might need to add an hour in the summer (BST). Check the tide tables you're using.

TIDAL RANGE

The difference between high and low water is called the tidal range. Spring tides will go higher up the beach at high tide and lower at low tide. Extra-low tides can cause problems—check out your favourite beach for rocks and mud!

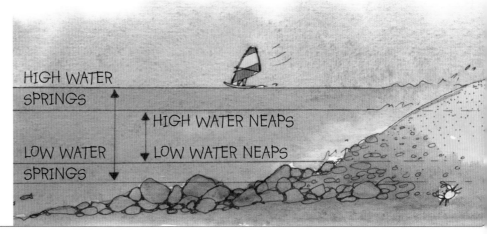

HIGH WATER SPRINGS

HIGH WATER NEAPS

LOW WATER NEAPS

LOW WATER SPRINGS

ON THE BEACH

"Well, it was here last time I came!"

A gently shelving beach can look very different at low tide—you might have to carry your gear a long way!

Check out a new location at different times to see how it looks at high and low tide. Remember the tide goes out and comes in even further on a spring tide.

TIDAL STREAMS

All that water doesn't just go up and down; it has to move sideways too. This is called the tidal stream and it can be strong around headlands and islands, as well as in river estuaries. Tidal streams flow at their strongest midway between high and low water.

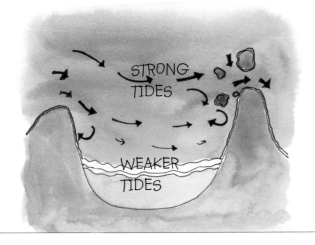

Stay tide aware—don't leave your gear unattended at the water's edge on a rising tide!

WIND OVER TIDE

If the wind is blowing one way and a strong tide is flowing the other, you can find yourself in some very choppy water.

Top Tip
To find out how the tidal stream is flowing, look at a fixed object on the water like a buoy or a moored boat and you'll see how the water flows past it.

A place that's good for windsurfing is likely to be good for other water-users too. So how do you avoid bumping into somebody? There's a highway code for the sea called the International Regulations for Preventing Collisions at Sea—and it applies to every type of boat, from windsurfers to big ships. Here are a few you really need to learn...

"EVERY VESSEL SHALL AT ALL TIMES MAINTAIN A PROPER LOOKOUT"

This is the most important rule of all. It sounds easy to do, but if you're concentrating hard on your stance and the position of your sail, you can sometimes fail to notice that you're about to crash into someone...

Yippee!

OVERTAKING

An overtaking vessel has to keep clear of the vessel being overtaken—whether it's big or small, sail or power.

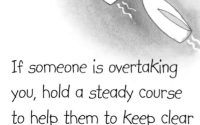

If someone is overtaking you, hold a steady course to help them to keep clear of you.

PORT GIVES WAY TO STARBOARD

If you are sailing on port tack, you have to give way to someone sailing on starboard tack.

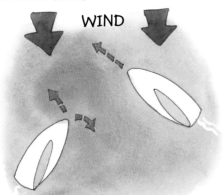

WIND

WINDWARD GIVES WAY TO LEEWARD

What if you're on the same tack as the sailor you're trying to avoid?

Think about where the wind is coming from. The upwind board must give way to the downwind board, like this...

WIND

Get to know your sailing area and avoid busy places where ferries or yachts are moving around. Your eyes hold the key. Keep a careful **LOOKOUT** and if in doubt, keep out of the way.

POWER GIVES WAY TO SAIL

Usually, any boat under power (and that includes rowing boats and kayaks as well as boats with engines) has to give way to someone under sail...

BUT... not always. A windsurfer is the niftiest sailing vessel of all, so you have to keep clear of sail boats that would find a sudden change of course harder than you.

A windsurfer can sail in shallow water, but a yacht has a keel and may not be able to change direction without going aground!

WATCH OUT FOR SWIMMERS

Swimmers are hard to spot! At sailing centres, swimmers are usually kept in a separate zone, but on a public beach this won't be the case.

Top Tip

How do you know which tack you're on? If your left hand is at the front of the boom, you're on port tack. If your right hand is at the front, you're on starboard tack. How to remember? Well, right hand forward = right of way.

STARBOARD = RIGHT

PORT = LEFT —give way!

AVOID A COLLISION AT ALL COSTS! The most important thing to remember— don't bump into anything or anyone!

With careful preparation, you can stay out of trouble. But knowing what to do if things do go wrong is an important part of your training. Here are a few ways to get yourself out of trouble...

GETTING HOME DOWNWIND

If you're upwind and the wind is too strong, or you're too tired to sail, try **FLAGGING**.

Get into the secure position and lean the rig forward until the board and rig are pointing at the shore. Stand behind the rig with your feet either side of the mastfoot. The rig should be easy to balance with no power in the sail, and the wind will blow you gently home. Steer by tilting the rig side to side.

REMEMBER—this only gets you downwind! If the wind is blowing you further away, you'll need another approach...

IF THERE'S NO WIND TO SAIL—Try paddling the board in a **BUTTERFLY** (described on page 36) or, for longer distances, in a **TURTLE**. This will also work in light headwinds, but is not easy in choppy seas.

1. Kneel on the board and separate the rig from the board.

2. Pull the rig over your head with the sail on your back and the boom round your chest.

3. When you lie down on the board the mastfoot should be facing forwards and the boom clear of the water.

4. Now use your hands to paddle back to the shore.

Top Tip
If it's too far to paddle back to the place where you launched, aim for the nearest bit of safe land.

With good planning you won't ever have to get rescued—but make sure you know what to do if you can't get yourself home and have to summon help.

DON'T LEAVE IT TOO LATE

If you can't help yourself, don't leave it too late to ask for help.

GEAR FAILURE

A windsurfer is a simple piece of equipment, but remember to check it's in good order.

The **UPHAUL** gets a lot of use, especially when you're learning! Check it regularly for signs of wear.

The **OUTHAUL**, holding the clew of the sail to the boom, is another small piece of rope that can break.

Check the **MASTFOOT** regularly for signs of wear.

Check your **SAIL**—a small tear can quickly become a big one!

An experienced windsurfer will carry a spare length of line as an emergency repair for the outhaul or downhaul.

GETTING HELP

You've already learnt how to do a distress signal (page 36) by lowering and raising your arms, but there are a few other things you can do as well.

Wave a Dayglo flag or anything bright (like a hat). You can keep a flag tucked into the zip compartment of your buoyancy aid if there is one.

You can also use a whistle to attract attention, though remember that sound is always blown downwind!

Top Tip

Whatever happens, stay with the board. It will help you stay afloat and you'll be easier for rescuers to spot.

If you need to take a tow from a rescue boat, take the line through your towing loop and pass it back to the boat, or tie it securely. There are some useful knots on the next page.

There aren't many ropes on a windsurfer, but everyone who goes on the water needs to learn a few *basic* knots. Whether you're helping out with the rescue boat at your club, taking a tow, or need to make a temporary repair to your outhaul, these should do the trick...

FIGURE OF EIGHT

A stopper knot, usually tied at the end of a rope to stop it slipping through a block.

Make the shape of a number 8 on its side...

...then bring the free end through the loop and pull tight. It should look like this...

ROUND TURN AND TWO HALF HITCHES

Useful for tying a rope to a post or mooring ring.

Loop twice over the post and bring the free end round into two half hitches. Pull tight and it will look like this...

REEF KNOT

Everyone is familiar with this one—for tying two ends of rope together (as long as the ropes are the same thickness).

All you need to remember is 'left over right and under, right over left and under'.

BOWLINE

This is a useful one for putting a loop in a rope.

1. Twist the rope into a small loop like this...

2. Bring the free end through the loop and behind the standing part...

3. Then bring the free end back into the middle like this...

If it doesn't end up looking like this, you've gone wrong somewhere. Have another go!

If the weather's not right for going out on the water, get hold of some spare line and practise knot-tying. See who can tie all four of these knots the fastest!

WHAT NEXT?

- Windsurfing theory

- Windsurf fast

- Start racing

- Beach start

- ...and stop!

- Windsurf clever

- More-advanced gear

- Fastfwd

So now you're hooked on windsurfing, and spend more time than you should gazing out of the window watching the wind rustle the leaves on the trees and dreaming of the next time you can get out on the water.

As you gain confidence, windsurfing gets faster and more exciting. You can learn to use a harness, get planing in strong winds, take part in racing, or learn amazing freestyle tricks.

This chapter gives you a few ways to begin taking your windsurfing to the next level...

You don't need to understand the science behind windsurfing to be good at it—but it can certainly help. And you'll impress your friends if you can talk about the centre of effort and the centre of lateral resistance—especially if you understand what they mean!

HOW DOES A WINDSURFER WORK?

A board moves as a result of two forces— the wind pushing sideways onto the sail is resisted by the daggerboard, fin and length of board in contact with the water. The result, like squeezing a bar of wet soap between your fingers, moves the board forward.

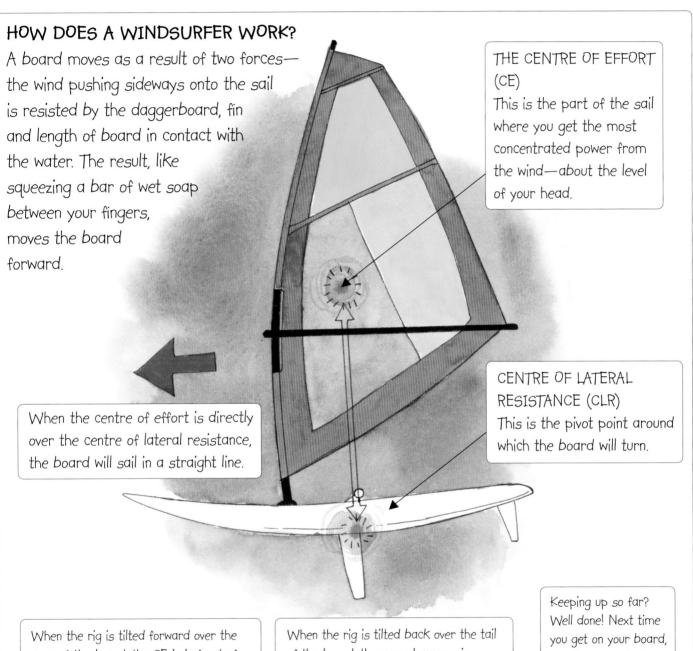

THE CENTRE OF EFFORT (CE)
This is the part of the sail where you get the most concentrated power from the wind—about the level of your head.

CENTRE OF LATERAL RESISTANCE (CLR)
This is the pivot point around which the board will turn.

When the centre of effort is directly over the centre of lateral resistance, the board will sail in a straight line.

When the rig is tilted forward over the nose of the board, the CE is in front of the CLR. This means there is more power over the front of the board than the back, so the wind will push the front of the board away from the wind (downwind).

When the rig is tilted back over the tail of the board, the same happens in reverse. There is more power over the back of the board, which will move downwind—pivoting the nose towards the wind (upwind).

Keeping up so far? Well done! Next time you get on your board, see if you can feel the CLR under your feet and the CE in the sail.

As you get more confident, you'll start to sail in stronger winds with bigger sails and experience the thrill of windsurfing at high speeds. From Youth Stage 3 onwards, you'll learn new techniques for handling higher speeds, and new equipment to help you fly...

PLANING

In light winds your board moves through the surface of the water a bit like a boat. But as you get faster something amazing happens. The wind lifts the board slightly out of the water and it skims over the sea. This is called planing. To see what this looks like, watch experienced windsurfers blasting across the water. To feel it for yourself—keep practising, get your stance right and you'll know when it happens by your increase in speed!

HARNESS

If you're worrying about whether your arms are strong enough to hold onto the sail in strong winds, don't panic. From Youth Stage 3 you'll learn to use a harness to help balance the sail with your body weight.

As well as taking the strain off your arms, the harness helps to transfer some of your weight from board to rig—which helps you keep control and go even faster!

GYBING AND TACKING

At planing speeds, you'll learn new tacking and gybing techniques and to make fast and smooth changes of direction without losing speed.

WHAT—NO DAGGERBOARD?

In light winds, a daggerboard adds extra grip, stops you slipping sideways and so helps you sail closer to the wind. But at planing speeds, when the board skims over the water, a daggerboard makes the board unstable. If you have one, make sure that you raise it at fast speeds or when sailing downwind.

FOOTSTRAPS

At fast speeds, TRIM—keeping the board level—becomes vital. Your legs and feet need to work harder to control the board. Footstraps help you to hold the perfect position for fast planing.

Top Tip

Fast windsurfing means you have to pay a lot more attention to your stance and react quickly to every slight change in the wind.

It's the next best thing to flying—and I should know!

A great way to test your skills is to take part in some club racing, as you can see how your technique compares with that of your friends. Racing is not just about going as fast as possible—the course will challenge all your new skills...

THE START LINE

Unlike the start of a race on shore, your start line on the water is going to be full of boards on the move! Try to get yourself in the best position to cross the line as soon as you can after the start gun has gone.

Wait for me!

If you cross the line before the gun goes, you'll have to take a penalty (this usually involves making a 360-degree turn or having to cross the line again).

THE COURSE

A typical course will be shaped like a triangle, to challenge you on all points of sailing. The course will be marked by buoys and you'll be given a briefing on shore before you start so that you know where to go. Look at where the wind is blowing in relation to the course, and what the tide is doing. Make sure you've got the best rig and board for the wind strength.

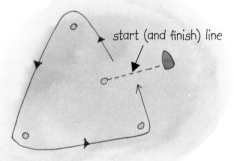

start (and finish) line

HAVE FUN!

If you just want to race for fun to improve your skills, club-level racing is always a great social event off the water as well as on it. A barbecue tastes all the better after a fast day's windsurfing!

Racing? Yes please!

If you're serious about racing, club-level fun races can lead to competing at regional, national level and beyond. Take it as far as you want to go!

Find out more about Team 15 clubs and their racing programme at www.team15.org.

THE RULES

Racing means close sailing with other boards, and there are rules for racing to help avoid collisions. You don't have to learn them all at once, but the rules of the road (see pages 52–53) are a good place to start.

KEEP CLEAR if you're the give-way board. Avoid collisions, and give another board room to get round a mark or obstruction.

Top Tip
If you're keen on racing, ask for a good waterproof sports watch for your birthday to help you count down to the start.

Starting and stopping get a bit smarter once you're more confident on the water. A beach start gets you sailing without all that uphauling—and it's a skill you need to learn as it prepares you for the even more impressive water start...

1. First things first—a cross-shore wind is best for a beach start. Don't wade out too deep to begin with. Position the board across the wind and stand on the windward side, towards the back of the board.

2. Get a feel for steering before you step on. To turn the board downwind, move the mast tip forward towards the nose by pushing down with the front hand, in and up with the back hand.

Turn the board back upwind by moving the mast tip towards the back of the board—push out with the back hand, pull in with the front hand.

3. The best position to start is with the board slightly upwind of a beam reach. Push the sail up above your head with both hands on the boom and place your back foot in the middle of the board.

4. Extend your arms so that the rig is as high as possible as you transfer your weight to your back foot.

5. As you step up, extend your front arm. It's important to keep your head down, 'nose over toes'.

6. Keep your head below the boom and eyes on the mastfoot until both feet are on the board and you've started moving.

7. Adjust your stance, face the way you're going and shuffle hands and feet into the sailing position. Off you go!

Top Tip
As you improve, try beach starts in deeper water, then see if you can have a go with your foot off the bottom. You're well on the way to a water start!

OOPS! What went wrong?

Catapulted over the front of the sail? Turn the board a little more into the wind to reduce power.

Can't get going? In light wind, turn downwind a bit to increase the power in the rig.

Falling off the back? Keep your arms extended and your knee bent as you step up. Remember—nose over toes!

Tee hee

LANDING WITHOUT MAKING A SPLASH!

Now you've learnt to step aboard and sail off in style, try coming back to shore like a pro...

1. Head upwind to slow down. When you get into shallow water, pull down the boom and step off with front foot first...

2. Then follow with the back foot and lower the rig. On a shelving beach, make sure the daggerboard is raised before stepping off.

Freestyle windsurfing is amazing to watch—a high-speed acrobatic dance of board and sailor that *looks* pretty much impossible. You can watch some fantastic video clips online and it's easy to think 'I'll never be able to do anything like that!' But don't despair—even the most expert freestyler had to begin where you did...

Now that's really showing off!

START SIMPLE!

Freestyle begins with tricks and challenges that you can try from an early stage. They get you moving around on the board—as a beginner you concentrate so hard on getting your stance right you can end up rooted to the spot! Start in light winds until you get more confident.

See if you can lift one foot up when sailing—then try dragging a foot in the water.

Take one hand off the boom... Then see if you can clap your hands whilst sailing!

Sail kneeling down—or even sitting!

When you get more confident, try spinning right round on the board. You can learn how to spin your rig 360 degrees too!

Try clew-first sailing... It's good practice for fast gybing techniques.

Top Tip
Get together with your friends and set a challenge—sail round a course seeing how many tricks you can do on the way.

When you get to the stage of wanting to buy your own board and rig, learn as much as you can about the different types so that you don't waste money on the wrong gear.

CHOOSING A BOARD

Board sizes are measured in volume, so you need the right volume board for your weight and experience. Too light a volume and you'll sink in low winds. Too high and you'll go slower than you need to!

The first board you buy will be a good all-rounder, with footstraps, that's the right size for your weight. Most intermediate and advanced boards don't have daggerboards.

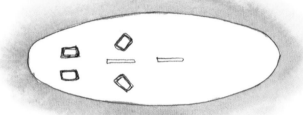

You'll also start to learn about specialist boards—like freestyle (small and light with a tiny fin) or freeride boards (perfect for high speeds in choppy seas).

SMARTER SAILS

An experienced windsurfer will have a selection of sails (a 'quiver') in order to choose the best one for the conditions.

Beginners' sails are fairly simple and easy to uphaul, but more advanced sails are called fully battened because they have battens all the way across to the mast.

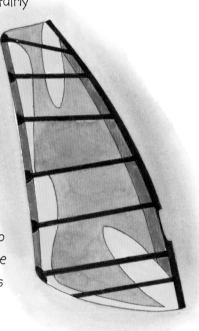

This means the sail will set into a wing-shaped curve to make the best of the air flow—which gives you more speed!

COVER YOURSELF!

As soon as you buy your own board and rig, make sure you get some third party insurance for it. This will cover you if you cause any accidental damage to another water user. The RYA gives free cover to windsurfing members—find out more at www.rya.org.uk.

Oops!

SERENITY

CLONK!

The more advanced your equipment, the more care you need to take setting it up and getting the rig tuning right.

As you progress, your instructors will get you to concentrate on the five basic principles of windsurfing. This five point check system is called Fastfwd and it's useful to remember at any level. If you're having difficulty, then one or more of these need looking at...

Whether you're a buoy or a gull, big or small, you can take your windsurfing to the next level. It's all about skill rather than muscle power...

GULL

BUOY

FASTFWD—
The five principles of windsurfing

VISION
The most important of the five. Use your head—look in the direction you're sailing.

STANCE
Remember you are part of the machine. The way you stand on the board and position your body is everything...

TRIM
Be aware of where you are on the board. Make sure your weight is where it needs to be to keep the board flat and in control.

POWER
This is about learning how to position the rig to get the most power out of the wind. Particularly important once you start planing!

BALANCE
Balance the weight of wind in the sail with your whole body, using your front arm to keep you at the right distance from the rig.

Don't get crabby if you keep falling in—pay more attention to the five principles...

There's nothing fishy about windsurfing—it's fast, wet and fun!

Come out of your shell—give it a go!

AMAZING WINDSURFING FACTS

- Who invented windsurfing?

- How fast can a windsurfer go?

- Where is the windiest place on earth?

- Can you windsurf across an ocean?

- What about windsurfing around Britain?

- How many people can you fit on a windsurfer?

- How high can a windsurfer jump?

- What about you?

Now put your feet up and enjoy a few pages of
amazing facts about wind and windsurfing...

Who invented windsurfing?

When is a sailing boat not a boat? When it's a windsurfer!

It's not easy to give a date for the first windsurfer, as Polynesian sailors centuries ago had board-like sailing boats that they steered standing up, but the first person known to have put a sail on a surfboard was American Newman Darby in 1948. The main problem was working out a way of steering the board with no rudder, and Darby worked out that a universal joint would be needed for the rig to be moved in all directions to steer the board.

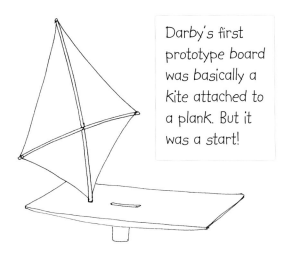

Darby's first prototype board was basically a kite attached to a plank. But it was a start!

On the other side of the Atlantic, an English boy called Peter Chilvers was sitting on the beach at Hayling Island in 1958 working out ideas for an early type of windsurfer, and he started to develop designs of his own. It wasn't until 1970 that Americans Jim Drake and Hoyle Schweitzer patented their own windsurfing design, which now included a wishbone boom and fully rotational universal joint. The sport of windsurfing—or boardsailing as it was also known—had begun!

Windsurfing became very popular in the 1980s and in 1984 was declared an Olympic sport. In the 1990s rigs and boards became very advanced and in the last decade or so new wide boards have made learning easier than ever thanks to RYA training schemes and the increase of windsurfing centres and activity holidays.

So get your wetsuit on and you can grow up to be one of the sailors who take the sport of windsurfing past its 100th birthday!

How fast can a windsurfer go?

At the time of writing, the fastest windsurfer on the planet is Briton Steve Thorp, who managed 50.48 Knots (93.4Km/hour) on 3rd January 2012.

Well, I *think* that was the world speed sailing champion...

Speed records are timed by GPS over a 500-metre course. Windsurfers first started taking on sailing boats at Portland Speed Week in 1975 when a strange-looking two-man board managed a respectable 13.5 Knots. The race was on—over the next 20 years windsurfers pushed sailing speeds to the limit, overtaking boats with their light weight and planing potential.

Who will be the next windsurfing record breaker? It could be you!

Where is the windiest place on earth?

Plenty of windsurfing resorts claim to be the windiest—which is not surprising as they all want us to go there!

Tarifa, at the Atlantic edge of the Straits of Gibraltar, has been popular with wind-seekers for a long time; so have the Canary Islands. Brazil is a hot spot for some really serious waves as well as wind, along with Maui in Hawaii.

Any guesses where the real windiest place on earth is? You wouldn't want to go windsurfing there—it's the coast of Antarctica, where the icy winds blow all year round and regularly reach 200mph. Brrr!

A Dutch windsurfer called Gerard-Jan Goekoop gave high-latitude windsurfing a try in 1985. He was the doctor on board a survey ship in the Arctic, and was able to give windsurfing in pack ice a go at 80 degrees north. Have a look at a globe to see how close to the North Pole this is!

Can you windsurf across an ocean?

Only if you are very tough and have a very special board. French windsurfer Raphaela Le Gouvello loves oceans, and has windsurfed across most of them on a 7.8-metre hollow board, which has enough space inside to store food and gear, and stretch out in a sleeping bag.

Her first ocean was the Atlantic—2,750 nautical miles in 58 days in 2000. Next was the Mediterranean, from Marseille to Tunis—a short sprint of 550 nm in 10 days. This was a warm-up to the big one—the Pacific; Lima (Peru) to Tahiti took 89 days at a whopping 4,500 miles in 2003. The Indian Ocean was next—3,500nm in 60 days.

OCEAN CHALLENGE FINISH

START

He's working up to it one step at a time...

The more time you spend on the water, the more you realise how fascinating and important the sea is.

Like many others who spend time on the water, Raphaela is a keen environmental campaigner and believes that knowledge about the sea leads to respect and understanding.

What about windsurfing around Britain?

Sailing across an ocean is one kind of extreme challenge, but sailing round a coastline is tough too—especially round Britain and Ireland, with over 2,000 miles of changeable weather, strong tides and rocky shores. The first windsurfer to tackle this was Richard Cooper in 1999, who took 61 days, windsurfing for 8 hours each day and then sleeping each night in his support boat. Richard was raising money and awareness for the Marine Conservation Society, and was shocked to find how much litter was in the sea around the coastline. More about the MCS at www.mcs.org.uk.

How many people can you fit on a windsurfer?

If you really want to sail with a friend, there are tandem boards with two masts—though you'd have to get your tacking and gybing down to a neat routine.

If you think sailing a tandem board would be tricky, imagine what it would be like sailing on a nine-man board! Dutchman Joop Nederpelt designed an 18-metre board with nine sails—now that would be really tricky to tack and gybe!

How high can a windsurfer jump?

Windsurfing on waves is a special skill, skimming along the crest of the surf and using the power of the waves to leap high and do spectacular tricks like full somersaults.

It's hard to measure how high a jump goes, but some are known to be up to 18 metres high—that's as high as a six-storey building! That's as close as you can get to flying.

What about you?

Windsurfing is constantly developing into new areas that would have amazed the early pioneers of the sport in the middle of the 20th century. You can windsurf fast, windsurf to win, fly off waves, invent new tricks or break world records that no-one else has even thought of...

Or you can just get out on the water and enjoy yourself. Whatever you choose, stay safe and have fun!

No, there isn't a world record for falling in...

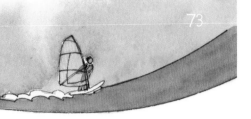

The bits at the back of the book

Don't go just yet—there's some useful stuff on the next few pages, as well as a bit of a quiz to test all your new knowledge!

- Quiz challenge

- How to find out more

- Sign up for a cleaner sea

- Answers to quiz

- What the words mean

- Wind and weather converter

There are going to be days when you can't get out on the water. Either there's too much wind, or not enough, and even the keenest windsurfer can't do much in bad weather. But you don't need to stare out of the window—get together with your friends and take the quiz challenge!

1. Why is an onshore wind better for windsurfing than offshore?

   ....

2. Do depressions circulate clockwise or anticlockwise?

   ....

3. Here's a compass rose—but the directions have all gone missing...

   - Put in as many points of the compass as you can

   - Which direction is the wind shown by the arrow?

4. How often does a spring tide happen?

   ....

5. How many hours are there (roughly) between high and low water?

   ....

6. If the forecast tells you a gale is due 'later', when would you expect it to arrive?

   ....

7. Do you know your rules of the road? Draw arrows to show which direction the give-way boards should go.

Which tack is which? Colour the boards on starboard tack red, and the boards on port tack green.

8. Name four things you can do to summon help or help yourself if you get into trouble.

1. ....

2. ....

3. ....

4. ....

9. Name five of the seven common senses.

1. ....

2. ....

3. ....

4. ....

5. ....

10. Name two things to watch out for when sailing close to headlands.

1. ....

2. ....

11. List two things you can do to keep control in strong winds.

1. ....

2. ....

Finished? Answers on page 78 (no cheating!).

About the RYA (www.rya.org.uk)

The Royal Yachting Association is about much more than yachting—it's the governing body for nearly all watersports, including windsurfing.

For more about RYA Team 15, go to **www.team15.org.**

RYA Publications

The RYA publish some great books on windsurfing (including this one!):

G49 RYA Start Windsurfing

G51 RYA Intermediate Windsurfing

G52 RYA Advanced Windsurfing

W1 RYA Youth Windsurfing Scheme Syllabus & Logbook,

G47 RYA National Windsurfing Scheme Syllabus & Logbook

(junior and adult log books to show your progression through the sport)

www.rya.org.uk/shop stocks all the publications if you want to buy online.

The Green Blue (www.thegreenblue.org.uk)

The Green Blue gives practical help and information on how to look after the sea—no-one wants to sail on a floating rubbish tip, and all watersports enthusiasts have a part to play in keeping the water clean.

The RYA and The Green Blue have produced a fantastic book about the oceans called 'RYA Go Green—A young person's guide to a blue planet'. It's the same format as this book (only with more sharks!)—big and colourful, packed with information and some very fishy jokes.

Clean water is vital, not just for windsurfers to sail on, but for the health of the whole planet. It's up to all water users to play a part in using the sea wisely—to be part of the solution not part of the problem! It's not difficult—here are a few guidelines to start you off...

Find out more about the water beneath your board from the Marine Conservation Society (www.mcs.org.uk) and The Green Blue (www.thegreenblue.org.uk).

- Never ever throw rubbish into the sea—even if it's biodegradable.

- Never leave rubbish on the beach—even if it's biodegradable.

- If you cook on the beach, use a disposable barbecue so that you can bag up the remains and take them away with you.

- Persuade your windsurfing centre or sailing club to sign up for recycling facilities—www.thegreenblue.org.uk has all you need to get things in place.

- If you're having a picnic lunch, don't feed the seagulls or ducks, however much fuss they make. Human food and rubbish is really bad for them.

- If you're involved in running the club rescue boat, make sure refuelling is done carefully and any spills mopped up. Even a small amount of oil in the water causes damage.

- Plastic waste is killing the oceans; carrier bags blow far out to sea and kill wildlife. Keep plastic bags away from the beach—and avoid those plastic tabs that hold packs of canned drinks together as birds get stuck in them and die.

- Get together with your friends and do a beach clean-up around your club—or join a national beach clean scheme.

- If you come across a stranded sea mammal on the beach (dolphin, porpoise or whale), alive or dead, don't touch it, but phone the RSPCA as soon as possible.

thank you

1. Why is an onshore wind better for windsurfing than offshore?

    An offshore wind is dangerous as it will blow you out to sea and make it hard to get back to shore once you start getting tired.

2. Do depressions circulate clockwise or anticlockwise?

    In the northern hemisphere, depressions (low-pressure systems) circulate anticlockwise. It's the opposite in the southern hemisphere.

3. Here's a compass rose—but the directions have all gone missing...

    The arrow shows a south-easterly wind.

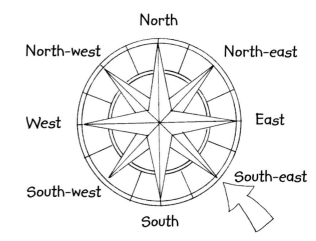

4. How often does a spring tide happen?

    About twice a month.

5. How many hours are there (roughly) between high and low water?

    Just over six hours.

6. If the forecast tells you a gale is due 'later', when would you expect it to arrive?

    After 12 hours (but never forget it's only an estimate!).

7. Do you know your rules of the road? Draw arrows to show which direction the give-way boards should go.

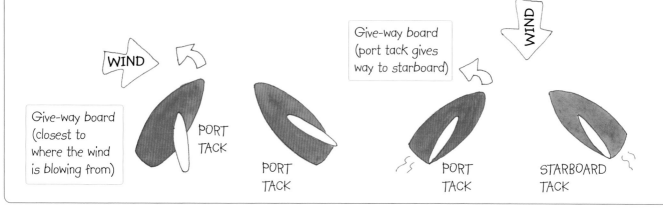

8. Name four things you can do to summon help or help yourself if you get into trouble.

1. Wave a Dayglo flag or brightly coloured piece of clothing.
2. Move your arms slowly up and down.
3. Blow a whistle.
4. Use flagging—see page 54—but remember this only works downwind.
Can you remember the other methods of self-rescue? Check out pages 36 and 54.

9. Name five of the seven common senses.

1. Is all your equipment seaworthy and suitable?
2. Tell someone where you are going and when you will be back.
3. Obtain a weather forecast for the local sailing area.
4. Are you capable of handling the prevailing conditions?
5. Windsurf with others.
(You can also include: avoid strong tides, offshore winds and poor visibility; consider other water-users.)

10. Name two things to watch out for when sailing close to headlands.

1. In tidal waters, you can get strong tidal streams around rocks and headlands.
2. If the cliffs are high, watch out for sudden strong gusts of wind from all directions (including vertically!).

11. List two things you can do to keep control in strong winds.

1. Change to a smaller sail size.
2. Bend your back knee to lower your body weight (particularly useful when steering downwind where you feel more pull on the sail).

How did you do? Other things to do ashore when you can't go windsurfing could include:
- Challenge your friends to a knot-tying competition.
- See if you can work out wind strength and direction by feel, then check online to see if you're right.
- Check over your kit, including wetsuit and buoyancy aid; give it all a good wash in fresh water and check for wear.

Anticyclone	High-pressure weather system bringing settled, dry conditions.
Balance	One of the five principles of windsurfing—counterbalancing the weight of the wind with your body.
Balance point	The point where the sail is drawn across the board and feels light.
Battens	Stiff but flexible strips inserted into the sail to give it strength and shape.
Beach start	Stepping onto the board in shallow water with the rig part-raised, and sailing off without the need to uphaul.
Beam reach	A direction around 90° away from the wind.
Bear away	Turning the board away from the wind.
Beaufort Scale	Way of assessing wind strength by observation.
Blasting	Windsurfing fast!
Boom	The part of the rig you hold on to, to control and steer the board.
Bowline	The knot you use when you need a secure loop at the end of a rope.
Broad reach	A direction downwind from a beam reach, 135° from the wind.
Buoyancy aid	Personal equipment that helps you stay afloat—never go on the water without it!
Butterfly	A way of self-rescue—lying face down on the board and paddling with your rig lying at the back of the board.
Centre of Effort (CE)	The part of the sail where the power of the wind is most concentrated—about the level of your head.
Centre of Lateral Resistance (CLR)	The pivot point of the board around which it will turn. When the CLR is directly below the CE, the board will steer in a straight line.
Clew	The back corner of the sail—attached to the end of the boom.

Close hauled	Sailing at about 45 degrees to the wind—as close as you can get without going into the no-go zone.
Cross-shore	A wind that blows along the shore, parallel to the beach.
Daggerboard	Rectractable long fin that helps prevent the board being blown sideways.
Deck	Surface of the board—the part you stand on.
Depression	Low-pressure weather system bringing unsettled conditions.
Ease	Using your back hand to let the back of the sail out, decreasing the power.
Ebb	The tide going out.
Figure of eight	A knot you put in the end of a rope to stop it running through a block.
Fin	The bit that sticks down at the back of the board—helps the board to steer.
Flagging	A downwind rescue, letting the board and rig drift downwind without any pressure in the sail.
Flood	The tide coming in.
Foot	The bottom edge of the sail.
Footstraps	Found on intermediate and advanced boards to help you balance the rig in stronger winds.
Freestyle	Spins, jumps and all kinds of amazing tricks and moves on a board!
Gybe	A turn carried out away from the wind by turning the tail of the board through the wind.
Harness	A way of hooking on to the boom to help balance the rig with your body weight in stronger winds.
Head up	Steering the board closer towards where the wind is coming from.

Knot	A nautical mile per hour (a nautical mile is a bit longer than a land mile).
Leech	The back edge of the sail.
Luff	The front edge of the sail.
Mast track	The slot in the board to which the UJ is attached.
Mastfoot	Bottom of the mast—the bit that gets attached to the UJ.
Meteorology	The study of weather and weather forecasting.
Neap tide	Happens every two weeks—not as high or low as a spring tide.
No-go zone	The area 45 degrees either side of the wind where your sail won't work.
Nose	Front of the board.
Offshore	When the wind is blowing directly off the shore/land to the sea.
Onshore	When the wind blows from the sea directly onto the land. Tricky to get going, but at least you'll be blown back to shore!
Outhaul	Rope used to attach the clew to the boom.
Port	The left-hand side of the board (facing forwards). Port tack means the wind is blowing over the left side of the board.
Power	One of the teaching principles of windsurfing—it means positioning the rig to get the most power from the wind.
Reef	A knot to tie two ends of rope together.
Rig	The mast, boom and sail together—a windsurfer's engine!
Round turn and two half hitches	A knot used to tie a rope to a post or bollard.

Run	Sailing directly downwind.
Secure position	Standing with the wind across the board, getting ready to sail, holding the rig downwind so there is no power in the sail.
Sheet in	Pulling the back of the sail in with your back hand, increasing the power.
Slack water	A time when the tide stops flowing because it is about to turn.
Slalom	A race where you have to do lots of nifty turns around buoys!
Spring tide	Happens every two weeks—higher and lower than neap tides.
Stance	One of the five principles—the way you position your body on the board.
Starboard	The right-hand side of the board. When you are on starboard tack, the wind is coming over the right side of the board.
Tack	An upwind turn taking the nose of the board through the wind.
Tail	Back of the board.
Trim	One of the five principles—positioning your weight to keep the board level and in control.
Turtle	A self-rescue technique—similar to butterfly but with the rig detached and secured over your body by lying inside the boom.
UJ	Universal joint—the clever piece of kit that attaches the boom to the board and enables it to swivel in any direction.
Uphaul	The rope used to pull the rig out of the water—you get to use this far too often when you're learning!
Vision	Another of the five principles, and a really important one—the importance of using your head and looking in the direction you are sailing.
Water start	Advanced technique—getting straight up out of the water using the wind without having to uphaul.

WIND SPEED CONVERSIONS

You'll find wind speeds given in several different ways—Knots (nautical miles per hour), Kilometres per hour, miles per hour and Beaufort Scale. It's useful to be able to translate the speeds into Beaufort Scale so that you can assess what conditions will be like.

Here's a quick way of translating approximately from one measurement to another...

Miles per hour—Knots: Take off 15 percent (so a 20mph wind is 17 Knots, force 5). To make it easy, just remember that miles per hour is higher than Knots—m for miles is also m for more.

Kilometres per hour—Knots: Halve it. So a 10Kph wind is 5 Knots (force 2) but a 20Kph wind is 11 Knots (force 4).

BEAUFORT SCALE

(more about the Beaufort Scale on page 20)

0 Calm	less than 1 Knot
1 Light Airs	1—3 Knots
2 Light Breeze	4—6 Knots
3 Gentle Breeze	7—10 Knots
4 Moderate Breeze	11—16 Knots
5 Fresh Breeze	17—21 Knots
6 Strong Breeze	22—27 Knots
7 Near Gale	28—33 Knots
8 Gale	34—40 Knots
9 Severe Gale	41—47 Knots
10 Storm	48—55 Knots
11 Violent Storm	56—63 Knots
12 Hurricane	over 63 Knots

GALE WARNINGS

Imminent—within 6 hours

Soon—6—12 hours

Later—after 12 hours

Get the full weather picture on www.metoffice.gov.uk.

Notes

Jot down your own notes and wind websites for your area...

Index